Counting your birthday

Lisa Bruce

Heinemann
LIBRARY

Little Nippers

www.heinemann.co.uk/library
Visit our website to find out more information about **Heinemann Library** books.

To order:
☎ Phone 44 (0) 1865 888066
▤ Send a fax to 44 (0) 1865 314091
▣ Visit the Heinemann Bookshop at www.heinemann.co.uk/library to browse our catalogue and order online.

First published in Great Britain by Heinemann Library, Halley Court, Jordan Hill, Oxford OX2 8EJ, part of Harcourt Education. Heinemann is a registered trademark of Harcourt Education Ltd.

Editorial: Jilly Attwood and Claire Throp
Design: Jo Hinton-Malivoire and bigtop, Bicester, UK
Models made by: Jo Brooker
Picture Research: Rosie Garai
Production: Séverine Ribierre

Originated by Dot Gradations
Printed and bound in China by South China Printing Company

ISBN 0 431 17190 4 (hardback)
07 06 05 04 03
10 9 8 7 6 5 4 3 2 1

ISBN 0 431 17195 5 (paperback)
07 06 05 04 03
10 9 8 7 6 5 4 3 2 1

British Library Cataloguing in Publication Data
Bruce, Lisa
Counting your birthday – (Maths all around us)
513.2'11
A full catalogue record for this book is available from the British Library.

Acknowledgements
The publishers would like to thank the following for permission to reproduce photographs: Gareth Boden.

Cover photograph reproduced with permission of Gareth Boden.

The publishers would like to thank Annie Davy for her assistance in the preparation of this book.

Every effort has been made to contact copyright holders of any material reproduced in this book. Any omissions will be rectified in subsequent printings if notice is given to the publishers.

2

Contents

1

One cake, baked and ready.

Two wibbly wobbly jellies.

Wibble

Wobble

2

Three

Birthday banners, up they go.

3

Four

4

Four bright candles for you to blow.

Five

Streamers for the party fun.

5

Six

With six prizes
to be won.

6

Seven

Seven biscuits on the plate.

Eight

Add one more and now there are eight.

8

Nine

Nine guests arrive,
all very excited.

9

Ten

Ten party hats make them delighted.

Hooray!

10

13

Eleven

PEEK-A-BOO

Hunt the hidden teddy bears.

11

14

Twelve

Everything ready
for musical chairs.

12

Thirteen

13

How many presents can you see?

Fourteen

Fourteen cakes for the birthday tea.

14

Fifteen

How many drinks on the table?

Count them all if you're able.

15

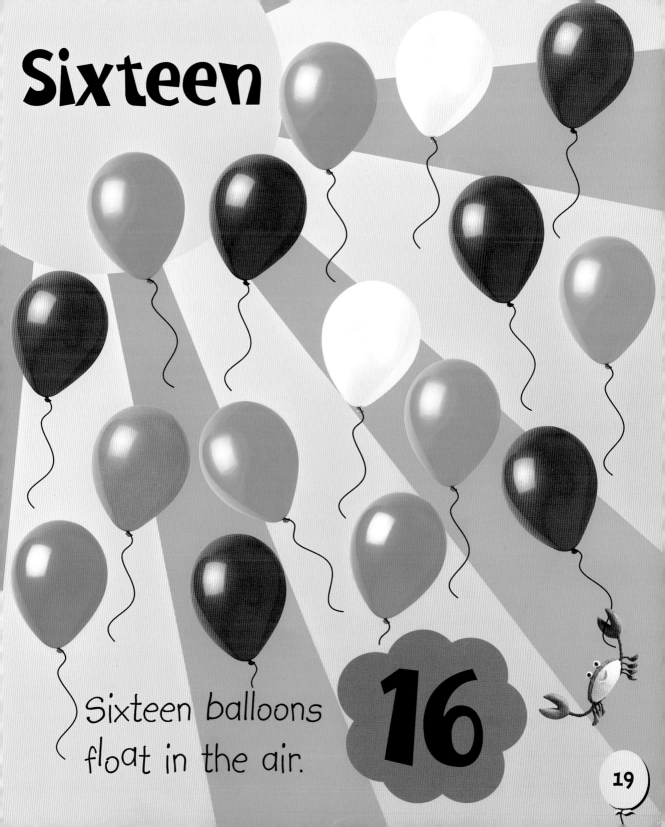

Sixteen

Sixteen balloons
float in the air.

16

Seventeen

Seventeen sandwiches cut into squares.

17

Eighteen

Eighteen sweets laid out in pairs.

18

Nineteen

Birthday cards all in a row.

19

Twenty

20

Bye bye!

Party bags, it's time to go.

Index

The end

Notes for adults

Maths all around us introduces children to basic mathematical concepts. The four books will help to form the foundation for later work in science and mathematics. The following Early Learning Goals are relevant to this series:
• say and use number names in order in familiar contexts
• count reliably up to 10 everyday objects
• recognise numerals 1 to 9
• use language, such as 'more' or 'less', to compare two numbers
• talk about, recognise and recreate simple patterns
• use language, such as 'circle' or 'bigger', to describe the shape and size of solids and flat shapes.

The *Maths all around us* series explores shapes, counting, patterns and sizes using familiar environments and objects to show children that there is maths all around us. The series will encourage children to think more about the structure of different objects around them and the relationships between them. It will also provide opportunities for discussing the importance of maths in a child's daily life. The series will encourage children to experience how different shapes feel, and to see how patterns can be made with shapes.

Counting your birthday will help children extend their vocabulary, as they will hear new words such as *banners, candles, streamers, prizes, delighted, musical, balloons, sandwiches,* and the numbers from one to twenty.

Follow-up activities
• Try to recreate some of the scenes in the book. Make party hats from cardboard for an imaginary party. Ask how many guests should be invited and make enough hats for them all. Take some of the party hats away and ask the children how many are left.
• Put up four banners instead of three and ask how the picture differs from the real thing.